Pit Ponies

by

Mike Kirkup

Ponies and their drivers coming to bank at South Pelaw Colliery.

Previous page: 'At the end of a hard shift there's nowt better than a nice soak.'

Back cover: Colour painting by Bill Hindmarsh.

Copyright Mike Kirkup 2008

First published in 2008 by

Summerhill Books
PO Box 1210
Newcastle-upon-Tyne
NE99 4AH

Email: andrew_clark@hotmail.co.uk

ISBN: 978-1-906721-01-5

Introduction

It was often said that ponies working underground were better looked after than those on the surface pulling milk carts and used for other various delivery purposes around the colliery villages of Durham and Northumberland.

Certainly, the underground stables were kept immaculately clean with each pony in a separate stall, bedded down with peat moss, and able to feed from a manger kept well stocked with a mixture of chopped oats, mixed vegetables and straw.

Each stall had the pony's name chalked on a board at the entrance, such as in this photo where, top left, the pony's name is 'Dancer'. Each animal was given a short name when it went underground, usually at four years of age.

Typical names were Star, Jet and Champ: names of one syllable that lent themselves to be shouted out in times of emergency, perhaps in front of a fall of stone. I used to act as a guide at Woodhorn Colliery Museum and the first place on site that I took children to were the stables on the surface. It was there I showed them around the four stalls, each with a pony's names chalked on a board. I asked them what would happen if a pony had a

There was one horse-keeper employed for every 15 ponies.

long name like Marmaduke. It took a while before the penny dropped, but then some bright nine-year-old would say: 'Because the pony wouldn't stop as quickly as a pony with only a short name.' Correct.

There was a stable for each underground seam, such as Beaumont and Brockwell, Middle Main and Low Main, each housing about eighty animals and looked after 24 hours a day by experienced horse-keepers. A farrier was called in regularly to see that the horse-shoes worn by each pony were in a good state of repair. The shoes, incidentally, were made by colliery blacksmiths on site.

Equipment worn by each pony when working, such as collar and safety headgear to protect its eyes from flying stones, were hung on the opposite wall. The height of these typical stables is adequate to house even the biggest pony which might be 14 or 15 hands, that is almost two metres, but the average height of a pony would be far less than that: perhaps only 9 or 10 hands.

Life was hard and dangerous for a miner hewing away in tiny underground tunnels, but that was how he chose to make his living. Not so the pit pony that was whisked away from an open field of lush green grass into a life of stones and coals, drudgery and darkness.

Mike Kirkup, June 2008

Mike Kirkup holds a pony's collar while former miner-cum-teacher Jimmy Slaughter gets a grip on a pair of limmers at Woodhorn Colliery Museum surface stables in 1992.

The Story of Coal

I sit on my seat with my whip in my hand
And I crack it so often and loud,
That the King on his throne and the Lord of the Land
are neither more happy nor proud.

That was part of a poem written by a thirteen-year-old boy working down a coal mine over a hundred years ago. It suggests that the lad loved his job working with a pony.

And it was no different from the generations of pit lads who followed their fathers, uncles and brothers into a life underground. It was what they had been brought up to do. For many there was no other choice.

Hewing coal was a back-breaking, tiring job, hacking away at the hard coal face with a steel pick. The roof was supported by steel planks held in place by wooden pit props.

This seam of coal is barely two-foot thick and the hewer was forced to kneel in this position for hours on end.

Once sufficient pieces of coal had been sliced off the face, it was thrown by means of a shovel into a tub which held about 12 cwt (just over half a tonne).

But the coal was no use sitting in a tub one hundred metres below the ground. It was vital to fuel trains and boats and factories where it provided steam to work the machinery that was just beginning to enhance British Industry in the mid 19th century. It was needed to keep families warm and to provide heat for cooking on an open fire.

So how did the contents of that tub of coal the hewer had filled come to be delivered outside a customer's door or at a woollen factory? Well, the first step involved using a pit pony. Pit roadways back then were never very high: sometimes as low as one metre. No machinery had been invented then that was small enough to be effective when it came to haulage direct from the coal face.

But in the 1920s, longwall faces replaced the single-place filler, and coal tumbled from a conveyor belt into the tubs.

This is an earlier photo that shows how NOT to hang a hambone on to the rope. The boy should be standing outside the rail tracks so that he doesn't get run over. You can see that there were two levels: one for empties (or chummins as they were called) and the other for full tubs. This photo on the left was obviously taken before it became compulsory to wear a safety hat; that happened in 1936.

Ponies were ideal for working in the barrier end of a coal face where it was quite low. Some ponies were tiny – as small as ten hands. A 'hand' is a unit of measurement for every type of horse, whether it is a huge Shire horse or a tiny Shetland pony.

Ten-hands is a little less than one metre high – an ideal height for working underground. Pit ponies might have been small but they were tremendously strong. They had to be, pulling half-tonne loads of coal underground on a narrow-gauge railway track of anything up to a mile.

One of the most prestigious jobs for a young man working down a coal mine was that of a putter. Here we see a typical putter with his slush cap worn at a jaunty angle, shirt collar outside his jacket – all the fashion in the 1950s – and a carbide lamp clipped to his lapel. Almost always with a smile on his face, this Jack-the-Lad character was usually the life and soul of any party.

Being on piecework, he had more money to spend than most of his marras still toiling away on the endless rope haulage system, hanging on and knocking off with an imitation baseball bat.

Putters were paid by the number of score (20) that they were able to 'put' either from a solitary or pair of fillers on an arc-wall face. But the lads still relied heavily on the type of pony with which they had to work. A good gallowa was worth an extra ten bob note in the putter's pocket on a pay-day Friday, whereas an ornery beast could make a misery out of the shift of any putter.

When the pits had first started in north-east England in the middle of the 19th century, most of the ponies used by local collieries were bred on farms in Ayrshire, Scotland. One particular breed came from an area called Galloway, and the ponies soon became known as 'Gallowas'. Because of their height, they were ideal for hauling coal and timber along the low, narrow workings which riddled the pit like rabbit warrens.

Once a putter had hitched his trusty pony on to the coal tub with a pair of limmers – wooden shafts in the shape of a yoke – it was ready to pull away. With a command such as 'Getton,' Roy,' the pony pulled and strained until the pair reached their destination at the 'landing' where other young lads were doing the same kind of work. The tubs were then coupled together, usually in sets of four, and were now ready to be despatched to the bottom of the shaft to await their ascent into the daylight.

It was easy for impressionable young boys to feel sorry for ponies in the underground stables as they never came to the surface, not even for a week's holiday in the summer. Even though young pit trainees thought this most unfair, a fourteen-year-old boy had no say at all in the way the pit was run. That was left to the wealthy coal owners who dominated the industry from positions of power, many of them as members of parliament.

Some owners held titles, such as the Duke of Portland whose land covered most of the east-Northumberland countryside. In Durham it was the Marquis of Londonderry who owned many acres of land. Portland owned Bothal Castle on the outskirts of Ashington, while Londonderry had a country mansion, called Wynyard Hall, which is now in Cleveland and at one time was owned by Sir John Hall who was a pitman's son, living in North Seaton Colliery Village until the 1950s.

Before young lads were allowed down the pit they had to serve for a few weeks on the dreaded Screens, an occupation that could be deemed as toiling in Hades itself. Most of the permanent workers here were either old, infirm or would be termed in those days as mentally retarded. The noise coming from the rumbling steel belt and the impact of stones and coal dropping out of hoppers at the far end was too much to bear.

Gaffers here would walk along that gangway contraption at the rear and point to you. Once he had gained your attention, he'd then stick a finger in his gob. This was the signal that it was your turn to get half an hour's respite in the canteen away from the chaos that was the Screens.

After the full tubs had come up the shaft they were marshalled on the heapstead then directed toward the tipplers which then dispatched their contents – whether it be stone or coal – on to the Screen belts. There was not supposed to be stone in these tubs and if any were detected then that weight would be deducted from the particular face-worker who had filled the tub in the first place.

Once the coal had been screened it was filled into railway wagons capable of carrying over 20 tonnes. Here we see a busy Ashington pit-yard in the 1930s with dozens of wagons carrying thousands of tons of coal to destinations far and near. A lot of coal was exported

via the staiths at Blyth, but a great deal went on the domestic market, mainly the concessionary coal that was delivered to colliery house owners who lived locally.

Each colliery had its own depot where private coal merchants filled coal by hand into Hessian sacks ready to take them to their customers. Most folks stayed loyal to one merchant, such as Geordie Nichol seen here on right with charge-man Geordie Charlton in the 1960s at Duke Street Coal Depot, Ashington.

Duke Street (named after the Duke of Portland) was where the first Fodens were used by Ashington Coal Company. Each lorry had four or five compartments which held just over half a tonne each of coal to be delivered fortnightly to miners' families in the district. Depot manager Jimmy Little's son is seen behind the wheel.

Household coal was literally dumped on the doorstep of a miner's colliery house. Youngsters vied with each other to 'hoy' the black diamonds into the coalhouse or cree.

Coal was an essential commodity in every household. It was what kept the kitchen-cum-sitting room warm and heated the oven where bread and stotties were baked and shanks of pork roasted. It was the one room where family members could congregate and chat about the events of the day. It was here that every young lad heard about working underground from his father or elder brothers.

Mike Kirkup says: 'I finished school on the Thursday before Good Friday in 1949. When I got home from school my mother said: "Michael, yor tea is on the tyeble. By the way, ye are startin' the pit on Tuesday!" I was fifteen. In four days I went from being a schoolboy to becoming a man.'

Without coal to boil hot water, the miner would have had nothing with which to wash himself. The collier had a superstition that if he ever had his back washed then that would take away his strength, rather like Samson having his hair cut. For modesty's sake, he usually wore a pair of football shorts. It was a demeaning ritual for a man to be seen undressed in full view of his family, and one which he endured until the first colliery baths were built. In Ashington that was as late as 1952. But some men still shunned the modern pit baths, preferring to walk home with the pit grime still embedded on their skin and their clothes thick with coal dust.

Horses for Courses

Bob Beach of Solihull came across pit ponies almost by chance, but he became fascinated by the tiny animals. Here is part of his research in words and drawings:

When I was quite small boy I remember that I went down the Nelson Pit at Cramlington with some Norwegian boy scouts for whom I was acting as a guide.

I recall pushing through some canvas ventilation doors in a cold, draughty and wet roadway with a narrow gauge railway line and then a man appearing from under our feet. He had just crawled out of a two-foot coal seam. I have no recollection of the pit ponies so, after a visit to Woodhorn Colliery Museum in 1995, I decided I would like to study them.

What breed were the pit ponies? Well, take the Highland and the Galloway, and add Shetland, Fell and Exmoor, Dartmoor and then Dorset ponies and Icelandic, Russian and Fjord ponies, don't forget Dales, Welsh Cobs, Cleveland Bays, Clydesdales and even Shires. In other words, 'Uncle Tom Cobley and All'. There were experiments made to produce tough little horses, but never a breed – the Pit Pony.

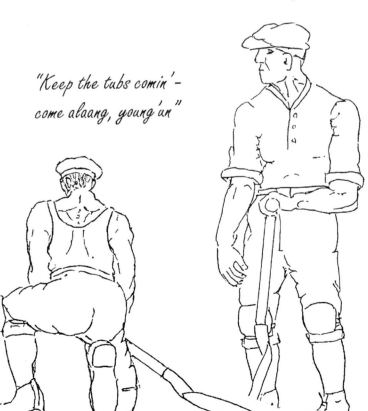

"Keep the tubs comin' – come alaang, young'un"

Different sizes of horse were required at different times at the actual colliery, let alone distribution by canal or in the famous four-wheeled London carts. On bank (above ground) it was general haulage before steam locomotives and winding gear took over. Turning the horse gins was exceptionally heavy work and the bigger the horse the better it could cope; 16 hands was about the lower limit.

In Wales, in the Valleys, outcrops enabled horses to enter and work drift mines. In the Midlands and Yorkshire, the coal lay deep underground; deep shafts and connecting galleries were needed to get to the coal-face, and horses had to be lowered down to them, at first by rope nets.

It was the largest of the coalfields in Northumberland and Durham which caused the real problems. In Durham in particular, seams were so thin that face-workers were forced to hew and fill coal into tubs, kneeling and even lying on their sides.

Putters, each with a pony, drove the full tubs outbye to the major roadways and returned inbye to the coal-face with chummins (empty tubs). These minor roadways had head-room only of three to five feet until the 'flat' (marshalling point) was reached, when larger ponies took over. The minor roadways (barriers) had twists and turns, points, brattices and gradients to negotiate.

Pit ponies used a draught collar, but the limmers (short shafts) were hung on their sides by a ridge chain and extra rump straps. The wooden shafts were joined at the rear by a semi-circular iron, which was attached to a lug on the tub by a cotteril pin (see diagram below).

Without doubt, pit ponies would have spent a more peaceful life in lush meadows, above ground, but working horses cannot exist without fulfilling an economic function. Of course, as always, there were good'uns and bad'uns. Good ponies were inclined to be overworked, but they probably led happier lives.

Some wore no bit, no reins or a single rein on one side, some were driven on long lines from behind the tubs. Many ponies formed bonds of friendship with their young putter lads. They would stand, patiently, waiting to be harnessed, or at points, or for doors to be opened which they themselves could open on the return journey.

Ponies would go slowly round sharp bends or over uneven rails, and would lean forward to help lift a tub after a derailment. They would stop at the top of an incline for the tub wheels to be locked (with a drag) and when the cotteril pin was removed would trot down to the bottom of the drift (hill) to wait for the tubs. They would back-up to tubs to be connected and even push tubs into line with the bottom of their collars. In complete darkness, they could find their way to and from the coal-face.

Many are the anecdotes told about their innate sense of danger and deeds of positive bravery which saved many lives. Many too, are the stories of individual habits: waiting for titbits at bait-time; some picking up a water bottle with their teeth before drinking the contents.

Some might turn around in the narrowest of roadways by half climbing up the walls; some would stop periodically for a rest, often in a restricted place where they could not be moved.

Since they greatly eased the burden of the men and boys to a remarkable degree, it is small wonder that many pit ponies were treated with both affection and respect.

'Ye Will Dee For Me, Bonnie Lad'

Mike Kirkup recalls his experience of pit ponies:

'First of all I was asked if I would like to go timber-leading. At that time in 1950 I was going on sixteen and had been working at the bottom of the Bothal Pit shaft since I had gone underground. Well, I thought I would give it a try, so I said Yes.

'My first job then was leading timber direct from the pit bottom to the Middle Main Drift. I was given Frank to work with – one of the most docile and obedient gallowas in the pit. It was beautifully marked with black and white patches from head to toe – or hoof if you want to be pedantic!

'Once I had got the tram-load of props to the bottom of the Drift they were taken over by three other timber-leaders who led their own tram or tub into the three coal faces that were operating then. It was strange for me at first because I had never even been close up to an animal before; that is if you don't count the pigs in my father's allotment which I sometimes had to feed with pig-swill made up of potato peelings given to us be our neighbours.

'But a pit pony … well … that was something to boast about to the Pont Street gang when we met up on the Hirst Park football ground on a Sunday morning. After about six months of leading timber and steel planks down the Drift, I was moved inbye – that is a little further towards the coal-face – to lead timber to a set of about ten fillers on a longwall face. That went fine and I got to know the burly fillers quite well, especially the guy at the barrier end whose job it was to hoy the timber and planks on to the belt after I had delivered them. An amiable chap called Latty was very appreciative and coming up to Christmas time he organised a whip-round with his marras and I was given a tidy sum of money. I found out later that this was a custom down the pit to reward non-pieceworkers. It was called something like Yale-Do. I supposed that the Yale bit was somehow connected to Christmas.

'There was an overman attached to each district and a deputy specifically working at each separate coal-face. Before long I found myself leading timber to two faces on the left side, not all that far apart but each with a different height of coal. This day I had just finished loading my tram with about two score (40) of assorted sizes from 3 ft to 3 ft 6 ins when the deputy on one of the faces came storming up to where I was loading with a face like Bela Lugosi. He took one look at what I had in my tram and exploded: "What the hell are ye loading these up for? Wor face only teks four-foots and upwards. My lads are waitin' on, dee ye knaa that? Ye are Kirkup aren't ye – wor timber leader?' With that he began to throw all the props I had loaded on to the ground.

"Aye, that's right, Mr X. But them props isn't meant for your face – it's for t'other one." By then I was almost in tears.

"Ye mean you're leading to *two* faces!"

"I nodded, sheepishly. "Oh, we canna hev that," he replied. "I will see that we have a second laddie in here pronto."

'And that is how I found myself working with Jimmy Brooks, a well-known character in the Ashington

Mike (far right, middle row) as a trainee at Ashington Colliery in 1950.

area. It was almost Christmas again, but this year I missed out on my Yale Do from Latty.

'I must have been spotted as a lad with potential cos after another few months had passed by I was asked by the horse-keeper in the Middle Main stables if I wanted to earn a little extra money by breaking in one of the new batch of gallowas that had just come down the pit. I think the going fee for this at the time was about one shilling (5p) a day. I have never been able to say No to any request, so I agreed.

'That is why I ended up one morning with Glen, a jet black pony with a ragged mane. I was not aware at the time that these new ponies were only four years old and, as such, were mere babies. To me, all ponies looked the same and had to be treated in a similar fashion. Wrong! Each of the animals I worked with was as different as chalk and cheese.

'But for a few weeks me and Glen got on well. I was pleased and so was the horse-keeper. Until, that is, the fateful day when it became time for Glen to be shorn of his lovely locks. I knew something was wrong the morning I saw the pony in his stall. In fact, I barely recognised him. All smooth and hairless he was.

'I managed to walk him inbye OK, but when I began to put the limmers on his back he went berserk; kicked and reared like a rodeo bronco. It was as though he was getting rid of all his inhibitions along with his hair. I never did get him to settle down that morning and the first time I turned my back, Glen was gone; literally done a runner back to the stables. It was weeks and weeks before I got him settled back into the regular routine. And all for a shilling a day!

'When I was eighteen I was asked if I would like to go coal-putting in the Bothal High Main. It was a natural progression for boys: from haulage to timber-leading to putting. Who was I to break the mould? So again I said Yes. If I had know what I was letting myself in for …

If you wanted proof that ponies worked for their 'choppy' then you just need to look at this photo of two old pals meeting up in the barrier. The dark pony on the left has obviously just completed a strenuous shift and his marra has just started work. You can tell this by the wrung-out-with-sweat mane on the bedraggled pony, contrasting the pristine dry condition of the other.

'Many of the lads I met on my first day's putting had either been on the same training scheme as me or I knew them from the football field. There was Alan Ford, Brian Blair, Alan Scott, Matty Taylor, Billy 'Buck' Brian, Spike Newman, Albert Savage, Jimmy Whitworth, Ray Logan, Billy Scott, Brian Middlemiss, Fred Armstrong, Ken Punton and Syd Morris, plus many others too numerous to mention.

'From the High Main stables – kept meticulously clean by horse-keeper Edwin Dodds – to our place of work was about a mile, and the ritual was that our gang of putters would ride the gallowas at a slow pace till we got to the 'flat' where we geared up the ponies with limmers etc. That first night – we were in the dreaded foreshift – as we rode inbye someone started up a song. It was Kay Starr's *Silver Dollar*. 'Oh, you can throw a silver dollar down upon the ground and it will ro ro roll, because it's ro ro round.' It was like being with Roy Rogers and the Sons of the Pioneers!

'But the sing-song was merely a brief interlude before the main event began. And that was more a horror movie than a western. I was putting to a one-man place to a fella that I already knew by name of Fred Athey, or Big Fred as he was affectionately known. Fred lived in Garden City Villas in Ashington and had an allotment near to my father's on Green Lane, and that is where I had first met him. Fred only talked and worked at one pace, and that was slow, believe me, that was slow. But as it turned out that was a blessing in disguise during that first shift I worked as a putter.

'It was quite a steep climb from that place and I had been given two ponies to work with – one to be hitched to the full tub and the other (called a tracer) to be attached to the stronger of the two animals. I don't recall the name of my pulling pony, but the name of tracer Bing will be engraved in my soul forever. He was a pint-sized bottle of dynamite! To get the empty tub to the face should have been a doddle. I only needed one pony for that, so Bing was hung on the coupling chain lug at the rear of the tub and only had to follow us to the working place where he could be unclipped and then fastened on with chains to the other gallowa to haul the full tub out. Clear? I thought not.

'We had only travelled twenty yards from the flat when Bing decided to dig his heels (sorry hooves) in, making the empty tub swing away from the rail track and upwards towards the roof. And all the while I am sitting on the limmers holding on as if I was on a rollercoaster at Blackpool. Inevitably, the tub was thrown off the way and we ground to a halt. I hoyed the chummin back on the way and started again. But Bing (name reminds me now of Chandler Bing from *Friends*) had other ideas and performed the same antics with the same results.

'To cut a long story short, I ended up by leaving Bing at the flat, taking the empty to Fred to fill, and then I had to push from behind to help my other pony to bring out a full tub. As the shift wore on I could hear the other lads bragging about how many tubs of coal they had 'put'. "Oh, I have got a dozen but my chap has not got into his stride yet." I closed my ears to the banter and took another tub back into where Fred was waiting patiently.

'At the end of the shift I could hear the lads comparing their totals: twenty-five, twenty-eight, thirty-one! And me? In an eight-hour shift I had managed to put a measly sixteen tubs. Sixteen! The shame of it all. But as I picked up what turned out to be my final tub that morning, Fred called out in a John Wayne-like drawl, "Aye, young Kirkup – Ye will dee for me, bonny lad."'

Jim Slaughter and Mike Kirkup swap yarns in a mock-up underground roadway at Woodhorn Colliery Museum.

If you think the weight of the equipment carried by the pony was extreme, that was nothing compared to the weight of a full tub of coals – 12 hundredweight in the 1940s – just over half a tonne in today's weights. This pony is pulling two empty tubs. The gallowa seems to be saying: 'Oh, come on there – you must be having a laugh!'

Ponies were aged about four years when they descended into the pit for the first time. After buying their ponies from Scotland, it was only a matter of time before the cautious Ashington Coal Company began to breed its own. The ACC owned large tracts of land which covered about five huge farms. Soon hundreds of ponies could be seen grazing on Coneygarth Farm. But a gentle, carefree existence in a green field under the north-east sun could only last for so long. Surface training began before the young ponies made that dreaded drop in the cage down into the bowels of the earth.

If the ponies faced a traumatic time on their first entry underground, then spare a thought for these terrified fourteen-year-olds lads with only a couple of metal bars to keep them from falling a thousand feet into the sump at the bottom of the shaft. Once the onsetter rapped on his bell, this cage, hanging precariously by a thin steel rope, would immediately propel them into a life that only those who have been there can fully comprehend.

As well as breeding the tiny ponies, ACC had a number of Shire horses that they used for a variety of things, such as leading concessionary coal to miners who lived in colliery houses. These gentle giants pulled tubs of coal along rail tracks that traversed every back street in the village. This painting by anon shows a Shire horse leaving the Hirst stables with the driver riding the limmers.

15

Training Ponies and Lads

Two young collier lads in typical pit attire about 1900 breaking in a pit pony to harness and coal tub on the surface prior to being sent underground to work.

Below are scenes of pony training in County Durham.

Training pit ponies at Tribley Pit, Hett Hills, around 1903. On the left is Mr Widderfield and on the right is William Rule. Ponies were trained on the surface of the pits where they were led around a dark circuit while pulling tubs.

Pit pony, training at Harton Colliery, 1912.

There were so many pieces of harness to put on the pony that it was difficult to know where to start. It was probably easier to begin with the stiff leather collar, stuffed to make it more comfortable to carry around the pony's neck during an eight-hour shift. The collar had short steel chains running from its sides to fasten on to another piece of equipment called limmers. Next came the bridle with its protective visor over the eyes and a steel bit to place in the animal's mouth to make it follow the young lad's barked instructions: 'Getton, Frank!' to pull, and 'Beah, Imp' to make it stop quickly. One pony at Ashington had a tender mouth and would not have a bit anywhere near it. As you can see, the two chains from the pony's collar were fastened on to a pair of wood and steel shafts, or limmers. These were kept in place by a leather belly-band that went around the animal's stomach. If you added the weight of all this equipment together then you have some idea of how strong a gallowa needed to be. See also that the wall behind was whitewashed, not what you would expect one hundred metres below the ground. And that pipe hanging above the trainees' heads carried the pit's electricity.

During their training, the lads were all under the supervision of an experienced old miner who taught them as much as he knew about working life below the ground. But there were some incidents that could not be foreseen and which inevitably led to accidents and sometimes sudden death. A gas explosion at Woodhorn Colliery in August 1916 resulted in the death of thirteen miners and a pony. John George Patterson, who was only twenty-one, was a stone-putter when he was killed along with his pony when methane gas exploded and brought down 70-yards of rock upon their heads. The Memorial at Woodhorn Colliery Museum (left) commemorates the names of the 13 dead men, but no mention is made of the pit pony. Perhaps it should have been. What do you think?

Pit Lads

Young lads who joined the industry in the 1940s were considered to be undernourished, so on the pit's 16-week training scheme were given half a pint of milk for free every morning in the pit canteen.

One of the sessions the lads liked best underground was when they were introduced to working with a pit pony.

Inside the canteen at Sherburn Hill Colliery, Durham, in 1949. Note the lads on the left sitting away from the 'men'. The canteen was replaced soon after this photograph was taken.

Hanging on a ham-bone to the trot rope. The pit had a vocabulary all its very own.

There was a lot to take in for a youngster who had left school with no qualifications at all to his name. It wasn't book-learning that was needed in a pit situation, but innate common sense. You only needed to bang your head off a low-lying steel girder to remember to duck the next time you passed that way. If you paid attention to what the older men had to say then the better chance you had to survive life underground without having a serious accident.

Boys in the 1930s and '40s were head-hunted by the coal companies with a view to becoming miners. It was a good deal for the owners as they got an extra pair of hands and paid very low wages for new recruits.

To entice a new work-force to come to the colliery, the ACC invited local headmasters to tour underground to see for themselves what it was like. Here we see a group of educationalists in 1939 in the pit yard at Ashington ready to descend in the cage. In centre with open coat is Michael McGough, head of St Aidan's Catholic School and on his left is Jos Gray, head of the Bothal School. Far left is mine manager Bill Gibson; far right is Mr Donald Hindson the agent, and 3rd right is Mr Joe Dockerty the Safety Officer.

The ACC in particular ran a high-profile public relations exercise by inviting well-known personalities to their colliery. One such celebrity was silent screen star Harold Lloyd who was appearing at Ashington's Miners Theatre for a week in the mid-1930s.

My Life Underground by Mark

"See me coming oot of the cage."

A Pit Pony Talks About Himself
From Ashington Colliery Magazine
January 1939

Aye, Aa can remember when Aa forst com' doon the pit. Aa didn't expect it t' be like Woolworth's basement. And mind it wasn't. But nivvor mind. Aa was takin' good care of, and Aa seun adapted messel'. Ye can see me in the forst picture coomin' oot of the cage.

Ivvorything seemed varry strange for a time, as was only natural, and Aa missed the moors and the heather and the open skies and racin' cloods and the champion feelin' of freedom as Aa used t' gallop through the grund-mists when they war aal golden in the sunrise.

Aye, but noo Aa'm weel cared for, and elwis get plenty t' eat. And ye can tell by the way Aa act, and be in the tip-top condition Aa'm elwis in, that Aa'm happy enough. And it's a fine thing t'knaa yo're dein' useful work in the world.

"Inta the forst left place."

In the second picture we're dein' away inta the forst left place. Aa knew it the time the filler in here wadn't be full. The same filler canna' fill a choppy box, and ye knaa we hev' ne time t' wait on men fillin' tubs.

Aa like pullin' tubs. Man, there's a keen pleasure in it. Yo're findin' expression for your health and energies, ye knaa, and like ivvorybody else in the world, ye get a big satisfaction in knaain' that yo're dein' the right thing with a willin' heart.

Mind, Aa divn't like bad-tempered putters – them that expect a powny t' read thor minds and t' knaa whaat t' de without bein' telt. Nebody can de that. When a putter treats me right and disn't get me feelin's aal worked up and jangly Aa can de me work champion and mek' it easier for him. But if he disn't, then it's warse for hissel'. Pownies are sensitive, and when they feel that people are not satisfied with them, they worry aboot it. But if the putter isn't the worryin' kind (and he shouldn't be) ye can bet that the powny hes an easy, happy mind, and enjoys his wark.

In the third picture ye see me oppenin' the trap door messel'. Aa can manage this nicely, and Aa divn't like people t' get inta me road. It might not be ony fun t' ye oppenin' a trap door but it is t' me. Aa enjoy that sort of thing.

"Oppening the trapdoor mesel."

"Askin' whaat he had in the bottle."

The putter's getting his bait in the next picture. He gov' us a scone and it was varry nice. Aa was just askin' him whaat he had in bottle when the photo was teun.

In number five, Aa'm comin' oot with the last tub t' mek' another score. The putters mek' me laugh when they brag aboot hoo mony scores they put. Whaat aboot the scores Aa put?

Aa canna' see ony sense in folks swankin' aboot whaat they de if they forget that they can de nowt unless other folks pull tigither with them. If Aa didn't pull tigither with the putter

"Whaat aboot the scores Aa put."

and didn't try t' be helpful, be gum, Aa'm sorry for the scores he wad put! And if he didn't help me Aa wadn't get much deun either. So there ye are. Nebody can de nowt on thor own. We aal depend on each other, and that's one reason hoo we should aal be fair and decent towards each other.

And in the last picture Aa'm ready to mek' a splash in the wesh-pond, and then trot inta the stables for a good feed of choppy. Ye notice the photographer? Ye canna even tek' your bath in privacy nooadays. Photographers are hingin' aboot like mistletoe at a New Year's Party.

"Canna even tek your bath in private."

Pit Pony Facts

Records from 1913 show that in the UK 70,000 horses were working underground. It was the peak of employment for horses underground. After that, as mechanical coal cutting and haulage systems became more efficient the use of pit ponies declined.

Horse transport could not keep pace with the increasing production of the new coal cutting machines and they began to be replaced by locomotives then conveyors. By the end of the 1930s underground pony numbers had declined to around 32,000.

Ponies up to 1.7 metres high or 16 hands were used close to the shafts, where many tubs had to be kept moving and the roofs of the haulage-ways were higher. Ponies up to 1.4 metres high or 13 hands were employed in the main roadways with their higher roofs. Ponies around 1.2 m metres high or 11 hands tended to be used near the coal faces.

Mining Memories

Thomas Failes from Willington remembers starting work in the hard times of the 1930s:

'I as one of the lucky boys who attended Bishop Auckland Grammar School until the age of sixteen. I was the eldest of seven children, and whilst my parents were quite happy for me to continue my education, I realised that money was far from plentiful. So, without their knowledge, I went to see the colliery manager and was promptly told to report to Oakenshaw Pit on the following Monday morning.

'I had to walk to Oakenshaw, I'm not sure of the time but it was quite early. On arriving there I was told to go to the shaft entrance where I was given a glenie (a safety lamp). My first drop in the cage was a very gentle one; a tradition reserved for a boy's first shift. From the shaft bottom I had to walk some distance to where the deputy was stationed, in what I can only describe as a small hut. My first job was to man a hand-operated pump; this I did sitting on a cracket (a stool). It was a very wet pit and water from the coal face ran into a sump, which then had to be diverted into another one. From there a mechanical pump was used to send water into the old workings. I had to be sure to regulate the flow so as not to overfill this second sump and if this did happen then I was shouted at.

A group of men take a break from working on the cages at Brancepeth Colliery 'B' Pit.

'One day during my first few weeks, when I went to check on the second sump, I stumbled and my lamp went out. I have never experienced such total darkness. Fortunately, I was near the track and was able to crawl along the rails to where the deputy was. The lamps were designed so that before they could be relit a rivet had to be removed and the only person authorised to do this was the deputy.

'At sixteen I started work at Oakenshaw Pit in the 1930s and after a few months I was given a new job. I was told to get a pony – his name was 'Bishop' but everyone called him 'Be-Sharp' – and fix him to a pair of shafts attached to a set of empty tubs.

'On asking what to do next I was told to sit on the front of the tub and the pony would show me. A few yards along the track, the pony stopped at what looked like a curtain, so I climbed down and pulled it to one side, wherein he moved on so I got back on the tubs.

Underground at Brancepeth Colliery in the 1930s.

'After a few steps he stopped again and I didn't know how to get him started, but then I thought that maybe he was clever enough to know that this curtain should be closed and as soon as it was shut off we went.

'I later learned that this was part of the ventilation system. Each time we came to another obstruction the same thing happened and eventually we arrived at what looked like a large cavern and here another boy unhooked the pony from the set of tubs and took it across to a track running in the opposite direction. Here it was harnessed to a run of full tubs.

'Off we went stopping and starting without me ever having to give any commands, taking me to the landing where full tubs were left waiting to be taken to bank. I must add that these ponies, although having to live underground, were very well cared for with their handlers becoming quite attached to them.'

The extract above was taken from 'Willington Remembered' by Olive Linge.

A pony and tub from Newton Cap Colliery. This is a postcard sent from Bishop Auckland on 25th July 1907 to Battersea Park in London. The message reads: 'One of the features of procession we had on Saturday last, pony and tub of coals. Hoping you are keeping well.'

Pit pony pulling a coal tub around 1906. It is decorated with awards won at the Bishop Auckland lifeboat appeal procession. Appeal processions were used to generate funds for hospitals and other services 100 years ago.

Bill Johnstone recalled his working days as a haulage lad and then a putter in 1922:

'The aim of haulage workers was to grow old enough to become a putter. A putter had to be eighteen years old and have a healthy strong body. His job was to drive the ponies that hauled the tubs of coal from the miner (filler) to the landings where they were assembled and attached to the haulage ropes. In the eyes of the young pit-lad this work carried prestige.

'Putters were on contract and could earn ten to twelve shillings a day (70p), which seemed a lot of money to us. At lunch-time, we haulage boys ate our lunch with the putters who recounted for our benefit of the dances they had attended, and the girls they had met and taken home. These stories were told with a lot of embellishment, and the lurid details of their romances often reached the point of absurdity ...'

'In January 1926 I was told I would get a cavil and become a putter. When the list of cavils was put on the notice board, my name was on it. It showed the section of mine where I would work for the next three months, and the name of the pony allotted to that section. The ponies didn't move from section to section each quarter as the men did, but worked in one place only. The reason for this was that ponies were of different heights, varying from nine hands (three feet) to

A Newbiggin pit pony with Ernest Punton at the head.

fourteen hands. It would have been useless to have a pony four feet tall allotted to a section that had a height of less than that. So the ponies stayed where they were best suited.

'These ponies were of differing temperaments too. Some kicked, some would not back-up, which was an essential part of the work, and some were stronger than others. A good pony could mean money to the putter who drove it. Local pits used three breeds: Shetland, Welsh and Galloway, as well as crosses of these breeds. The ponies were washed down at the end of each shift, fed chopped hay, carrots and grain, and bedded down in clean peat moss. Many people think that ponies were blind when brought to the surface, this is a fallacy. The ponies relied on the light of lamps, and their stables were lit at all times.

'A putter never referred to his animal as a pony. In Northumberland it was called a Galloway, regardless of breed. They were short, stocky animals, mostly of a gentle disposition, affectionate and responsive to kindness and a credit to the company that developed the strain.'

The extracts above were taken from Bill's book 'Coal Dust in my Blood'.

Good conditions here in the Main Seam stables at Pegswood Colliery from around 1952. From left: Harry Emery, hauler driver, John Brannan, Benny Burrell, and horse-keeper Billy Hindhaugh.

A pit pony with handler at New Herrington Colliery on 5th September 1907. The pony had worked for 26 years in the mine.

John Soulsby and Gordon Liddle with pit pony Fox in the Craghead Busty pit stables.

These ponies must have thought that all of their birthdays had come on the same day that they were released from the Busty Seam stables in June 1921 at Dipton Colliery.

A much more modern photograph of miners going to the baths at Eldon Drift, Shildon. These new pithead baths were opened by Sam Watson, Durham National Union of Mineworkers, on 11th November 1954, yet the drift closed in 1962.

Ashington Collieries' Pit Ponies At the Royal Show, Windsor

By Robert (Bob) J.S. Thompson, Lynemouth Colliery
from Ashington Colliery Magazine, July 1939

'We left Ashington bus station at 5.10 am on Monday, 3rd July 1939, by special bus for Newcastle and on arrival at Bedlington we picked up two more boys, arriving at the Central Station at 6.15 am. We saw men and boys at the station waiting for the early morning papers, and porters engaged in their daily work at 6.45 am. The train left for Windsor and we were given a hearty send-off by Mr Donald Hindson, Agent of Ashington Coal Co, Ltd and Mr Joseph Dockerty, the Safety Officer. Some more boys and their ponies joined us at Durham.

'After travelling all day we arrived at King's Cross at 4.15 pm. The engine was uncoupled from the train and we were stranded for four hours. After much telephoning we finally got an engine which took us the rest of the railway journey to Windsor.

'At 10.15 pm we arrived at Windsor, tired and in need of a wash. We were met at the station by a few officials and porters. We then proceeded through the dark streets of Windsor to the Park at which the Royal Show was being held. At once we fed and bedded the ponies down for the night. The boys then went to the dining tent where a hot supper awaited us.

'The next morning we arose at 6 am. We then fed and attended the ponies and exercised them. At 8 am the boys had breakfast. After cleaning the ponies' bridles we put the rosettes at the side ready for the visitors and the afternoon performance. We also attached cards around the ponies' necks with their names, ages and number of years worked underground.

'At 9 am the London people visited the stables and asked numerous questions about the ponies and if the boys stayed down the pit all the time along with the ponies.

'At 2.45 pm we proceeded to the Show Ring which was crowded with the interested spectators. On entering the ring the ponies and boys were loudly applauded by the crowd. Now and again a pony would rear on its hind legs, which caused amusement among the people.

'We paraded twice around the ring and then returned to the stables. We were then inspected by their Majesties the King and Queen, together with the two Princesses. Her Majesty the Queen asked my name and which Colliery I represented. On answering, His Majesty the King turned to the Queen and said that he had visited Ashington Collieries whilst he was Duke of York. The two princesses fed the ponies with sugar.

'After the departure of their Majesties the King and Queen, the crowd rushed to the stables to ask the boys what their Majesties had said. They were surprised

Back row from left: R.J. Thompson with Turpin; Sep Sweet with Spot and V. Riches with Noble. Front row: Edward Shaw with King; Fred Reavley with Jim and R. Stevenson with Geordie.

when told the ponies' eyesight was not affected by the pit darkness. At 4 pm tea was served to the boys and the ponies were fed and bedded at 6.45 pm for the night. On the last day of the show a microphone was brought into Windsor Park. One of the boys from each colliery was asked to broadcast his idea of London and the people. And then four of the boys, including myself, were selected to sing 'Blaydon Races.' We then retired and returned home on Sunday.

Some other boys on this trip had this to say, first Fred Reavley of Linton Colliery: 'On the Wednesday, the King and Queen (George VI and Elizabeth) came and were very interested in my pony, Jim, comparing him with their own, as they called it, pit pony. The Queen asked me if these were the clothes we wore down the pit. I said "Yes". Some of the people asked very silly questions. One old lady asked what were my physical reactions when coming to the surface after being down for three years?'

Ray Stephenson of Lynemouth Colliery said: 'Having been fortunate to be chosen to take Geordie, my pit pony, to the Royal Horse Show in Windsor Great Park, I think it was a great honour. The people who visited the Show had the idea that all the pit ponies were blind and ill-treated, but when they saw what condition they were in they said it was a credit to the horse-keepers who looked after them.
    'They thought that we pitmen lived in little tunnels down the mine all our lives. Each day we were allowed three hours off in which to have a look around the ground. During the day we wore our pit clothes and, being probably the first pit lads these people had ever seen, they stared at us so much that were glad to put our ordinary clothes back on.'

Ed Shaw of Ashington Colliery wrote: 'We had a lot of curious visitors all asking questions. "Are those pit ponies blind?" "What do they cut their tails for?" "Do you sleep down the pit with the ponies?" "Do you carry the coals out on your back?"
    'Anyway, we enjoyed answering them. The Princess Elizabeth gave the ponies some sugar sweets, and my pony, King, got a special pat from the Queen, and, of course, I was very proud of him. We had a good time and it let the people from down South see that the pit pony's life is not so hard as a lot of people think.'

Sep Sweet of Woodhorn Colliery wrote: 'Thursday was just another day of answering questions. On the Friday we marched around the ring in front of the two princesses (Elizabeth and Margaret), but the biggest thrill of all was meeting the King and Queen. I think the ponies had about a stone (6 kilos) of lump sugar. I wish the Show had lasted for six months!'

Finally, Victor Riches of Ashington wrote: 'I thoroughly enjoyed the experience of visiting the Royal Show with 'Noble' in my custody. The officials there and everyone we met were very sociable. We met hosts of ill-informed people, but they now know a bit more about pit ponies and their working conditions.'

Thirteen years later it was a Royal coming together in more ways than one in 1952 when Queen Elizabeth on her coronation year attended the Royal Show held that year at Newton Abbot. By sheer coincidence there was another 'Royal' appearing that day – it was an Ellington Colliery pit pony that had been selected out of the Group's stables as one of the animals to represent the north-east region at that year's Royal Show. On the right is Charlie Wilkinson, head horse-keeper at Woodhorn who retired in 1963.

Pit Pony Pal Goes to the Pictures

Little did a tiny pit pony called Pal think he would ever escape from the drudgery of life down Ashington Colliery. But when word went out that a pony was required to pull a cinema advertising cart around town, then Pal was brought out of the mine to take on a starring role. This beautiful chestnut with a silver white mane soon became a favourite with cinema-goers at the pit town's Miners Theatre in the late 1930s. The handler seen here at a Show in People's Park is cinema attendant Jimmy Harrison. The film being shown was *Strictly Confidential* starring Warner Baxter and Myrna Loy. But it was Pit Pony Pal who stole the show!

Pony Racing

Ponies rarely came to the surface, even for a holiday. It was tried, but the chaos caused when the dozens of animals had to be taken back down the pit resulted in that plan being shelved. Well, wouldn't you rebel against going into the blackness of a pit after a few days in the sunshine? That ban applied to all except the ponies with exceptional markings and temperament who sometimes surfaced for impromptu pony races. As seen here at People's Park, Ashington, in 1932. The races were part of an annual Agricultural Show where vegetables and flowers etc were displayed in the marquee on the right. Sideshows were provided for the children.

Right: An illustration by Bill Hindmarsh.

Bill hit the headlines in he 1950s when one of his paintings of life underground was chosen to hang on the wall of a famous industrialist. He worked as an electrician at Linton Colliery, but is now a full-time professional artist. Bill has an exhibition of his work planned for Woodhorn Museum in January 2009.

Putter lads always rode their ponies outbye to the stables at the end of a shift – it saved walking about a mile or more. Riding the ponies was illegal and in the 1950s was liable to a fine of five shillings, 25p. Once in a while the pit officials tried to catch lads riding the ponies. He hid in a man-hole at the side of the roadway carrying an overman's stick that was covered in white chalk. As the riders galloped past, the official would whack them on the back and then run as fast as he could to the bottom of the shaft. When the putter lads came to get in the cage to go to the surface, the overman inspected the coats of each lad and if there was a white slash on the back then that boy was fined. But the crafty putters used to turn their coats inside out when riding so no white chalk mark was visible. Clever, eh!

Here Bill Hindmarsh captures the excitement of a rare pit pony race at Peoples Park, Ashington.

The 19th Century

In the mid-19th century, to a pitman, going down a mine was as ordinary an event as nowadays taking the lift at one of Newcastle's sumptuous department stores. But to an educated man like William Howitt the whole experience was bizarre. Here is an extract of what he wrote concerning Monkwearmouth Colliery:

'It is a hot and fatiguing pit, but on account of its great depth it is the marvel of the district. At first you see little or nothing and it seems as if you were in total darkness. Then in a minute or two you distinguish the men at the shaft bottom, and the sluggish oil lamp, and the little lads coming up with their trains of Coal-waggons; then the horse and ponies, being unfastened from one load and conveyed inwards to draw another.

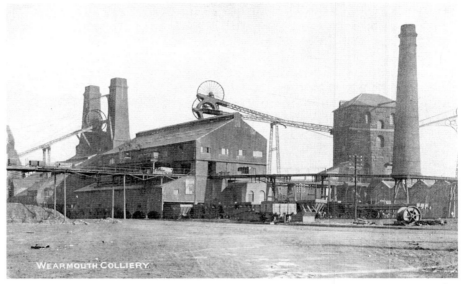

WEARMOUTH COLLIERY.

'Now you can see the remarkable smoothness of the horses' coats, and the sleekness of the ponies' appearance. The horse gets fat, the men lean, the ponies well-conditioned, and the lads ill-conditioned. The horses and ponies are conveyed down the pit in large nets; of course, they seldom get back up again, but live night and day in their underground stalls.'

Air Shaft, Wallsend

At Wallsend Colliery (etching by Thomas Hair) in the Church Pit in 1835, the most fatal explosion of hydrogen gas that had ever occurred in Northumberland was recorded when 101 men and boys lost their lives and four others were seriously injured. Eleven horses which were in the pit at the time were also killed.

A Royal Commission on Children's Employment reported its findings in 1842, shocking the nation with some horrific tales.

Nichol Henderson working at Monkwearmouth Colliery was described thus: 'Is bound as a putter, but unable to put yet. A year ago the horse ran away, knocked him off and he was trailed with the waggons. Off work for 10 months. Is lame now and will always be lame. One leg is shorter than the other.

'The pit makes him sick. The sulphur rising up the shaft as he goes down makes his head 'work'. Feels worse when he goes down at three o'clock in the morning; when he comes up at six in the evening he feels sick. It is nearly seven o'clock when he gets home.'

Alexander Bell, a putter, had the following reported by the Commission: 'Went down Walker Pit when he was nine years old. Was a healthy boy, is well now, generally, but is sometimes bad in his inside. Sometimes cannot walk well for this pain. Monkwearmouth where he works now is a very hot pit; hotter than Wallsend, Hebburn or Walker.

'They all work quite naked (except the drivers, trappers and flatmen) with the exception of a front covering of flannel and shoes. The putting is hard but the hardest thing is the heat; and the hours are long; has been lamed twice, rather bad. Can read an easy book. Writes his name. Does not go to night-school, but sometimes goes to Sunday school.'

William White went down a Northumberland Pit in 1859 and reported this:

'By and by we turned from the mainway into a branch level, narrow and low, where you cannot stand upright, and where ponies and not horses draw the waggons. Loose heaps of coal lay about from which men and boys were loading the waggons, and the ponies drew off one short tram after another, along the crooked and uneven tramway to the mainway.'

All extracts taken from 'The Great Northern Coalfield' by Mike Kirkup.

You needed brute strength to be a hand-putter, straining every muscle in your body to push the full tub, as seen in another of Bill Hindmarsh's evocative paintings.

A Dangerous Place

Unfortunately many ponies were killed while going about their daily work. Top of the accident list was getting caught between rolling tubs of coal.

Mike Kirkup was only fifteen in 1950 when he and his pony Frank were involved in an incident with a runaway cutting machine that left the animal with injuries to its leg, fortunately not life-threatening. He said: 'I was guiding a cutter on a flat bogie down the steep Middle Main Drift in the Bothal Pit. All of a sudden it began to run away with me and bore down on Frank who realised what was wrong and set off at a gallop down the steep incline. But the heavy steel machine caught up with him and knocked Frank over. We were both lucky to get out of that in one piece.'

Harry Hodgett's pony was not so lucky. He said: 'I was leading timber props into a tub-height barrier at Choppington Pit when the first thing I knew of any danger was when my gallowa dropped to the ground. It was so narrow that I couldn't get to it.

'I ran outbye to fetch the deputy who came running and went up to examine the pony's head. Without warning, the pit official dropped to his knees gasping for breath. There was a pocket of methane gas there which was invisible to the human eye.

'I got out of there as soon as I could, but the pit deputy and my pony were not so lucky. Both of them died in that incident. It was a brave thing for the deputy to do: to risk his life for that of a pit pony. But miners loved their animals so much that this man thought nothing of risking his own life in an attempt to save a pony.'

Ponies usually went down the pit aged four years and lived perhaps till they were about twenty or thirty. In the early days of mining when there was no place for sentimentality, once ponies began to slow down and struggle to pull their heavy loads they were killed humanely as possible with a bullet to the head.

The dead animal was then unceremoniously bundled into a tram and despatched to the surface where the carcase usually ended up in a knackers' yard where its bones were boiled down to make glue. It was not a happy ending for a pony that had given the best years of its life in serving its young master.

Here is a no-nonsense poem that depicts the demise of a Gallowa in 1920.

Lines on a Pit Pony
By Henry Scott

At the gloomy pit-shaft bottom
  His worn-out carcase lay,
A poor despised creature:
  A worked-out Galloway.
His gaunt old frame was thick with scars
  Which showed where wounds had been,
And told a vivid tale of woe,
  Of suffering long and keen.

What weary miles of stony road
  Had trod those little feet?
Each step with hard and dreary toil
  And misery replete.
His sole caress, a driver's whip
  His sun a candle-light.
His only joy a bed of wood
  To gain a brief respite.

But when his days of toil were done,
  His usefulness all past,
The friendly bullet laid him low
  And brought relief at last.
Not his lot of smiling fields,
  A short reward to reap.
When his long working days were o'er
  He was not 'worth his keep'.

One Memorial that does commemorate the dangerous work of the underground ponies is in the shape of a horse-shoe inscribed: '86 pit ponies suffocated at Ashington Jan 12th 1913'. Nothing seems to be known about this tragedy as it does not appear to have been reported in the local press. But something catastrophic must have occurred to result in such mass suffocation.

The Rescue

At the Hobson Pit, Burnopfield around 1966, without warning the earth opened up near the stables swallowing up a pit pony named Jack. It was caused by a cave in of a mining tunnel below the surface. Although the pony sank to a depth of about twenty feet, miners were able to bring Jack to the surface uninjured. Pictured here are some of the miners, many of them not in their work clothes, having either finished their shift or prior to changing for their oncoming shift. The men risked their lives during this act of great compassion. The ground may have opened up even further.

The pony is steadily reaching the surface and seems remarkably calm. The man on the right of the group hauling on the pulley ropes and wearing a white shirt is Anty Scott.

Safe at last and at home. Jack with miner Walter Hall. The pony seems none the worse following its ordeal.

Story and photographs from 'The Turnpike Road – Sunniside, Marley Hill & Byermoor' by F.G. Newman with Sunniside Local History Society.

Odd Tails

Cartoonists in the 1920s and '30s often depicted scenes where there was conflict between the deputy overman and the young putter lad, as seen in this 1926 illustration from the Ashington Colliery Magazine. Note the pitmatic dialect which was often difficult to decipher when written down.

There were a number of miners' strikes in the 1920s when men and boys rebelled against the low wages and poor conditions they had to endure. Pit pony images were used by the coal owners in attempt to shame the men back to work, as in this David Yarrow illustration below.

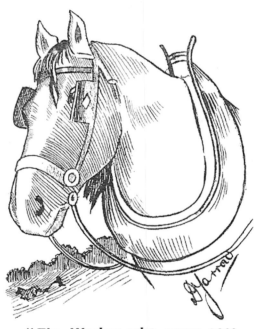

"The Worker who never goes on Strike."

The Ashington Collieries Magazine   350   November, 1926

THE BETTER WAY.

This illustration on left – also from the ACM – shows how pit pony drawings were used to represent the coal owners and the men. It seemed that both sides were pulling in opposite directions and that neither could exist in perfect harmony, even though both camps wanted to achieve the same goal: to feed from the bag of Prosperity.

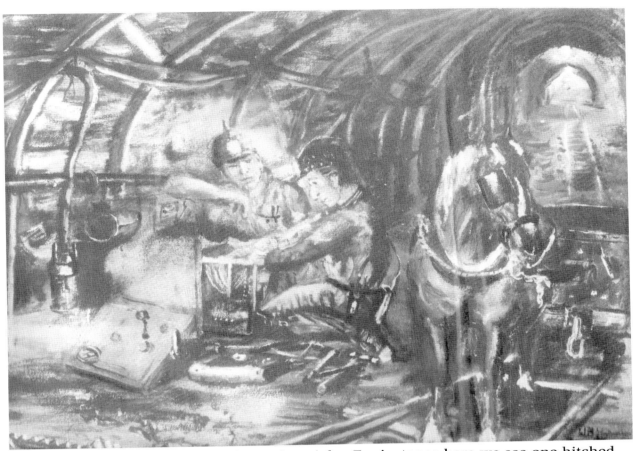

Ponies were used underground for various jobs. For instance here we see one hitched on to a tub that has been used for carrying electrical equipment for the two electricians, seen in this illustration by Bill Hindmarsh. All along the roadway, steel arch girders support the roof. Bill says he was trying to depict a road leading into eternity. After a year or so these girders would become twisted under the heavy strata bearing down from above.

Mr Dixon and Golightly with a pony at Hedley Pit, County Durham. The writing on the tub says: 'Plenty coal for the man who burst the pipe.'

Shire Horses

Shires and the Middens

These strong and willing giants were called upon to do all kinds of work around the pit-yard, such as hauling heavy machinery to the top of the shaft before it was despatched underground.

But one bizarre task the colliery Shires needed to perform was enacted at many pit villages in the dead of night. This was when the 'midden-men' got to work and cleared out all the outside privies (middens) of colliery houses.

This excrement was thrown into tubs and hauled away by the Shires to a nearby farmer's field where it was said the biggest potato harvest ever known came about as a direct result of the application of midden manure.

In the timber yard at Seaham Colliery in 1947. Left to right: Jack Hays, John Williamson, Ernie Rowell, Brian Corkhill and Harry Mortensen.

Stella Coal Company employees delivering coal to Rockwood Hill, Greenside.

Lads riding bare back at Chester Moor. Third from the left is Norman Forster. The main North Eastern Railway Line signal box is to the left.

End of Horse Power

Geordie Phillips has the distinction of being the last horse-keeper at Woodhorn Colliery. Said Geordie, who is now aged in his mid-eighties: 'I began as a putter at Woodhorn in 1938. After a spell on filling, I developed a beat knee so I was set on as an assistant horse-keeper in the Yard Seam stables where they had 125 ponies – there were 80 in the Low Main stables. 'When the pit was set to close in 1981 they brought all the ponies out and most of them went to Ellington. But four were kept to work on the surface at Woodhorn: Rod, Brig, Smokey and King, seen with me here in this Jack Wallace photo. The ponies were taken down the pit each day to help the salvage workers.'

Last day of working at Cambois Pit in 1968. Pit pony Craster is with Alfie Gibbs.

Pip, one of the last working pit ponies in the Durham coalfield left Sacriston Colliery after closure. He is seen here pulling a tub with one of his handlers Bill Tubman at the entrance to the Mahogany Drift mine at Beamish Museum. When Sacriston Colliery closed in 1985 seven pit ponies found new homes. Sandy, Smokey and Darkie went to Ellington Colliery, Pip moved to Beamish Museum, Bobby and Topper went to the Carlisle Animal Rest Home and Matt went to live with a private individual.

Photograph from 'Memories of Sacriston' by Dorothy A. Rand and George Nairn.

Out of the darkness of Ellington No 2 Pit and into the light at the surface – Flax, the last pit pony to emerge from Britain's pits, is handled in the cage by farrier/horse-keeper Keith Adams as shaftsman David Ure and banksman Kevin Anderson lay down a makeshift walkway. Three hundred years of horsepower came to an end at noon on 24th February 1994.

Keith Adams faces the media and tells his story on the pony's life underground at the shaft top, Ellington.

Many of the gallowas were real characters. One named Honesty pinched water bottles from pitmen's bait bags and drank the contents. Glitter refused to work

until given a baccy twist to chew. Fly would dance to his handler whistling a sea shanty. Tim survived a rock fall and walked with a limp when expected to work yet was fine when he thought no one was around.

Craftsmen watch the ponies emerge from No 2 Pit. Left to right: Joe Nichols, John Robinson, Neil Dixon, David Ure and Joe Hogg.

Jackson Reay (right) worked at Ellington for almost forty years, ending his days on salvage work. He is saying goodbye to pony Tom one of the last four to be brought out of a British Mine. Paddy Mellon, surface engineer, is centre.

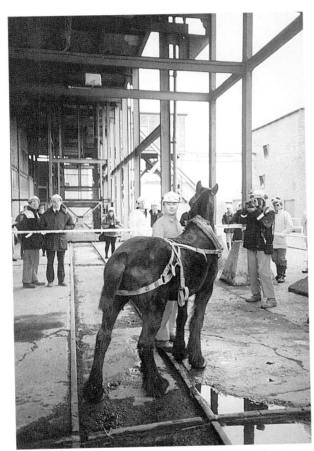

Keith Adams with Alan one of the last ponies at Ellington. Gallowas had an uncanny sense of impending danger and would sometimes refuse to move – saving pitmen's lives from a roof fall.

Keith in front of the Big E with Flax, a fourteen-year-old Welsh mountain pony who came to Ellington in 1983. At 12.1 hands high, he was described as a steady pony with a good temperament – ideal for working down the pit.

The extract above was taken from the article 'The Big E' by Neil Taylor.

Bill Hindmarsh painting of a weary pair, man and beast, making their way outbye at the end of another uneventful shift.

Acknowledgements

The author would like to thank the following who have helped with the publication of this book:

Beamish North of England Open Air Museum, Johnnie Briggs, Lena Cooper, Reuben Daglish, Thomas Failes, Derek Gillum, Jack Hair, Alan Harrison, Bill Hindmarsh, Tom Hutchinson, Mike Ingoe, Tom Jones, Olive Linge, Pamela Linge, Evan Martin, George Nairn, Francis & Margaret Newman, Dorothy A. Rand, Sunniside Local History Society, Neil Taylor, Sharyn Taylor, Jack Wallace, Trevor Williamson, Woodhorn Museum.

Bibliography

Ashington Colliery Magazine, 1923-1940
Andrew Clark, *Mining Memories*, 2002
Andrew Clark & George Nairn, *Durham Coal – A People's History*, 2001
Derek Gillum, *Out of Darkness Came Light*, 2005
Alan Harrison & Jack Hair, *Stanley Remembered*, 1999
Tom Hutchinson, *Shildon and District*, 2003
Bill Johnstone, *Coal Dust in My Blood*, 1993
Mike Ingoe, *Greenside Remembered*, 2007
Mike Kirkup, *Coal Town*, 1995
Mike Kirkup, *The Great Northern Coalfield*, 1999
Mike Kirkup, *A Creeful of Coals*, various dates
Mike Kirkup, *The Five Collieries*, 2000
Olive Linge, *Willington Remembered*, 2002
Evan Martin, *Bedlingtonshire Remembered*, 1999
F.G. Newman and Sunniside Local History Society, *The Turnpike Road*, 1998
Dorothy A. Rand and George Nairn, *Memories of Sacriston*, 2004